"Can we find anyone like this man, one
in whom is the Spirit of God?"
                    Genesis 41:38 NIV

JOSEPH
The Boy Who Learned to Handle His Dreams
Retold by Ben Alex
Illustrated by Philippe Pauzin
© Copyright 1988 by Scandinavia
Publishing House, Nørregade 32, DK-1165 Copenhagen K.
English-language edition published 1989
through special arrangement with Scandinavia
by Wm. B. Eerdmans Publishing Co.,
255 Jefferson Ave. S.E., Grand Rapids, Michigan 49503
All rights reserved
Printed in Hong Kong
ISBN 0-8028-5032-4

2

Joseph

The Boy Who Learned to Handle His Dreams

Retold by Ben Alex
Illustrated by Philippe Pauzin

Eerdmans

ook! Here comes the big dreamer!" Joseph's brothers said scornfully. They had just sat down in the green grass to eat their supper when they caught sight of Joseph.

It was easy to spot Joseph, even from far off, because of his bright-colored robe.

Joseph's older brothers did not like their little brother. He was their half brother and much younger than any of them. The other day he had caused trouble when he told their father that his brother Judah had taken a nap while watching the sheep.

Their father, Jacob, seemed to fuss so much over Joseph. He always took Joseph's side because Joseph was the firstborn son of his favorite wife Rachel.

At Joseph's recent birthday their father had given Joseph a beautiful, bright-colored robe with pockets and long sleeves. Since then his brothers felt Joseph thought he was too important to take care of the sheep. He stayed at home with his little brother Benjamin, the only other child Rachel had had. They played together all day long, while the older brothers stayed with the sheep. It was a hot and tiring job. They thought Joseph would never grow up to become a real shepherd. He usually sat around and daydreamed. The older brothers felt their little brother was a failure, and they did not know what to do about it.

Besides, Joseph talked too much. The brothers hated his bragging. He always seemed to be dreaming about something big. Even their father had to correct him sometimes.

Last week Joseph had told them about a dream he had. "Listen," he had said. "I had a dream last night. I dreamed we all were binding bundles of wheat in the field. Suddenly my bundle rose while your bundles gathered around mine and bowed down to it. Isn't that interesting?"

The next morning Joseph had described yet another dream. "Listen, brothers! I dreamed that the sun and the moon and eleven stars bowed down to me. Isn't that interesting?"

The brothers did not think so.

Reuben was especially worried about his little brother. Reuben was the eldest of the brothers. He looked forward to being head of the family someday when their father died. Even though he sometimes worried that Joseph might prevent that from happening, he still cared for his little brother.

Reuben shaded his eyes with his hand and watched Joseph running towards them. Then he turned to his brothers. "Listen, I have an idea," he said. "Let's teach Joseph a lesson he'll never forget. We'll throw him into the old dried-up well over there." Reuben pointed at the hole in the ground where the brothers had hoped to find water a few moments earlier. A couple of hours in the well might humble his little brother, Reuben thought.

"Great idea!" said Levi.

"Yes," grinned Judah. "That may cool him off."

By now Joseph had reached the brothers. He stopped to catch his breath. "You . . . are sure . . . hard to find," he began. "I've been walking all day. Father told me you were at Shechem. When I arrived there a man told me you'd gone on to Dothan. Father told me to find you and report back to him how you're doing with the sheep. I'm sure glad that. . . . "

Before Joseph could finish, Judah and Simeon grabbed his arms and held him while the other brothers tied up his arms.

"Hey listen!" yelled Joseph. "I'm your brother! Judah, get off my toes! What are you . . . ? Aghh!" A big hand over Joseph's mouth finally silenced him. His eyes bulged as he started to realize what his brothers were doing.

The brothers threw Joseph down into the dark well.

At first Joseph could see nothing at all. But gradually, as his eyes got used to the dark, he could see the stone walls rising round him. The floor was slimy and clammy. He shivered. He hated snakes and scorpions and lizards. About ten feet above his head he could see his brothers' heads against the sky in the narrow opening.

"Dream yourself some great dreams down there!" grinned Levi. Then the heads disappeared and Joseph was left alone.

he brothers finished their meal on the grass near the well. Tonight was Reuben's turn to watch the sheep. After the meal he went off to the field and left the brothers at the well.

"I watch the sheep. You watch Joseph," he said as he left.

Before long, Judah saw dust clouds far away. A caravan slowly approached them from the north. "I've got an idea," he whispered. "Why not sell Joseph to the caravan merchants? Then we'll get rid of him."

The others agreed.

"Slave for sale! Slave for sale!" From the well Joseph heard the shouting. He could also hear the hoofbeats of camels and donkeys.

"They're going to sell me!" he gasped. "They're really going to sell me! We're not playing games anymore! Father! I wish Father were here!"

But Joseph's father was far away, at home in Mamre at Hebron. There was no way he could hear his favorite son's cry for help. And Reuben was not there to stop the brothers' plan.

So, Joseph was sold by his brothers to the merchants. "He seems to be a strong and handsome boy," said the merchants. "We'll pay you twenty pieces of silver for him."

Then the caravan left with Joseph.

When Reuben returned from the pastures he realized what had happened. "Are you crazy?" he yelled. "What are we supposed to do now? How will you explain this to father?"

All the way home the brothers tried to come up with an answer. Finally, they decided to kill a goat and smear the blood on Joseph's bright-colored robe. They would tell their father Joseph was killed by a wild animal in the wilderness.

Father Jacob wept for many days when he heard the story of Joseph's death. "My poor son is dead," he mourned. "I shall cry till the day I die."

Little did Jacob know that some day, many years from then, he would get to see his dear son again.

9

In the meantime, Joseph arrived in Egypt. Night after night he had cried himself to sleep on the dusty caravan trail, not knowing what was going to happen to him. He knew he had been sold as a slave. He also knew how slaves were usually treated.

Some were put to work in the horrible copper mines. There they worked every day, nonstop. Most of those slaves died in the mines. Others became oarsmen on the Egyptian battleships. Most of those soon drowned or were killed. Others became brick-makers or metalworkers. They were whipped and tortured. Joseph would never be a free man again. The rest of his life, though probably very short, would be spent doing nothing but endless, tedious chores.

Joseph shivered at the thought of it.

Now the caravan entered a huge city in Egypt. For a moment Joseph forgot about his hopeless future. When they crossed the Nile River, the fantastic pyramids of Egypt rose in front of him. He had never seen anything like it! He was used to tents and sheep. This was wonderful! The majestic buildings, the crowded streets, the beautiful sculptures, the enormous pyramids! It was another world, even more exciting than the world of his childhood dreams!

"Hey, you . . . come here!"

Joseph was startled back into remembering why he was there. The merchant dragged him to a nearby marketplace. There he spoke to a big fat Egyptian, but Joseph could not understand what they said. Then the Egyptian placed Joseph on a little platform in the street, together with some other slaves. The fat Egyptian shouted and made all kinds of gestures to attract people's attention. Joseph guessed he shouted the same words his brothers had shouted at the well at Dothan, "Slave for sale!"

J oseph was sold to a wealthy Egyptian named Potiphar. He was an important man. He was the captain of King Pharaoh's bodyguard. He looked stern and kind at the same time. Joseph soon learned that Potiphar meant to use him as a house servant. He would not have to waste away in the copper mines! Joseph sighed in relief. "Thank You God," he whispered. "I know You will watch over me!"

Joseph worked faithfully for Potiphar. He even worked harder than he was asked to. One day Potiphar said to Joseph, "Joseph! I'm very pleased with the work you do. You are a skilled and honest young man. It seems like you have the favor of our gods."

"The God of Abraham, Isaac and Jacob is with me," answered Joseph.

"Anyway," continued Potiphar, "I think I'll put you in charge of my entire household. From now on you shall be called my steward."

Now Joseph was free to walk all over Potiphar's property. He was given a beautiful new cloak. He made sure his master had his meals served on time. He ordered the food and made sure the house was neat and clean.

Joseph took pride in managing Potiphar's household. And in doing this, he was taking the credit for his luck instead of seeing it as a blessing from God.

One day, when Joseph was walking down the hall past the bedroom of Potiphar's wife, she approached him. "Joseph, why don't you come and sleep with me tonight? My husband is out of town."

Joseph knew this was wrong. How could he do such a thing when his master trusted him? Joseph ran down the hallway before Potiphar's wife could touch him. But the woman ran after him and managed to pull off his cloak.

Now she wanted to hurt Joseph because he had not done what she wanted. So, when Potiphar came home she lied. "My dear husband, something terrible happened while you were away. Joseph, your Hebrew slave, tried to force me to sleep with him. See, here's the cloak he left behind in my bedroom."

Potiphar believed her lies.

"Put this wicked Joseph in prison!" he told one of his soldiers. "Because he has done this, he will spend the rest of his life behind bars!"

As the heavy iron door slammed shut behind Joseph and the key turned in the lock, Joseph sat down on the wet and filthy floor and cried. Now he was back where he had started, and there was no way to get out.

"God," he sobbed, "why am I so unlucky? I've lost my family, my country, and now my job in Potiphar's house. Are You still with me? I trust You, Lord. I trust You'll somehow find a way to get me out."

In the dark prison Joseph did not dream at all. He realized he had put his trust in himself and not in God's faithfulness. "I am sorry, God," he prayed. "Help me to forget myself and my big ambitions. Help me to serve You . . . even in this horrible place."

So, Joseph began to serve the prisoners around him. Many of them were sick. He brought them water and helped them clean up their cells. He tried to comfort them with a few cheerful words and a smile. Everybody in prison liked him, and soon the prison warden gave him little jobs to do. "Joseph," he said, "I see you care for other people. I like that. Besides, I feel I can trust you. Your God must be with you in a special way. From now on you shall be overseer of the prisoners."

Among the other prisoners were two very important ones. One was King Pharaoh's former baker. The other had been in charge of filling Pharaoh's wine cup. Pharaoh had thrown them in prison because he did not trust them anymore. One morning when Joseph visited their cell they both looked very sad.

"What's wrong with you two?" asked Joseph cheerfully. "Did you have nightmares?"

"Actually," they answered, "we both had strange dreams last night, and we have no idea what they could mean."

"Oh," answered Joseph. Then he thought for a moment before he said, "Why not let God Himself interpret your dreams?"

"God?" asked the cup bearer doubtfully. "How can God do that?"

"Well," said Joseph. "Tell me your dreams. Maybe God will tell you through me."

"I dreamed," said the cup bearer, "that I saw a vine in front of me. The vine had three branches. Buds popped out and these buds blossomed right away. Then clusters grew on the branches and the grapes ripened. The next thing I noticed was Pharaoh's cup in my hand. I took the grapes, squeezed them into the cup and put the cup in the king's hand."

"All right," said Joseph, "here's what your dream means. The three branches mean three days. Within three days King Pharaoh will release you from the prison and make you his cup bearer again. Now do you have any reason to look so sad?"

"Wonderful!" the man shouted. "Joseph, I like the way you explained my dream! I only wish I could do something for you in return."

Joseph looked serious. "You can," he said. "You can tell Pharaoh about me. I've done nothing wrong. Yet my life is wasting away in this prison. Maybe Pharaoh will let me go."

"I promise!" answered the cup bearer.

Now it was the baker's turn to tell Joseph about his dream. "I dreamed," he said, "there were three baskets piled on top of my head. In the top basket were all kinds of cakes and bread I had made for Pharaoh. Suddenly the birds came and ate the cakes and the bread."

Joseph felt sorry for the baker when he explained his dream. "This is what your dream means," he said. "The three baskets mean three days. Within three days Pharaoh will hang you by your neck, and the birds shall come and eat your flesh."

Three days later it happened exactly as Joseph had said it would. The cup bearer was back at his old job. The baker was killed.

But two years passed and Joseph still did not get out of prison. The cup bearer had forgotten his promise.

One morning as the cup bearer filled Pharaoh's cup with wine, he noticed the king did not look well. "Is anything wrong, your Majesty?" he asked.

Pharaoh sighed. "I had two strange dreams last night," he answered. "I'm going to call all the wise men of Egypt, tell them about my dreams, and see if they can explain them to me."

But the wise men could not give Pharaoh any answers. They just stood there, the priests, the fortune-tellers, the dream interpreters and the magicians. They looked so important in their beautiful robes, yet all they could say was, "Strange!"

"Peculiar!"

"Interesting!"

Then the cup bearer remembered Joseph. "Your Majesty," he interrupted, "in the prison there is a Hebrew slave who once told me the meaning of a dream I had. Maybe he can explain your dreams."

So Joseph was commanded to appear before Pharaoh.

"I've heard about you," said Pharaoh. "You're supposed to be good at interpreting dreams. Now tell me what my dreams mean."

"Your Majesty," answered Joseph, "I cannot interpret dreams. But God can."

"Anyway," continued Pharaoh, "here's what I dreamed. I was standing on the banks of the River Nile. Out of the river came seven fat cows. They began to graze on the banks. Then seven thin cows came up and ate the seven fat cows. Afterwards I had another dream. I saw a grain stalk with seven good and healthy heads of grain on it. Then seven other heads of grain sprouted on it. But

they were thin and scorched by the east wind. Finally the thin heads of grain swallowed up the seven good heads. Now tell me the meaning of these things!"

Joseph looked at Pharaoh. He took a deep breath. Pharaoh looked so frightening as he sat on his throne, impatiently waiting for Joseph to answer. What did the dreams mean? Would God tell Joseph?

Joseph cleared his throat and began to speak, "Pharaoh's two dreams . . . mean . . . the same thing. God wants to tell you what is going to happen soon. The seven fat cows and the seven healthy heads of grain mean seven years. The seven thin cows and the seven thin heads of grain mean another seven years. God is warning you that after seven good years with bountiful crops and plenty to eat, there will come seven bad years with scant crops and severe famine in Egypt.

"Pharaoh ought to find a trustworthy and wise man to put in charge of the royal storehouses. This man must make sure enough food from the seven good years is stored so the people of Egypt can have enough to survive the seven bad years."

19

"Excellent idea!" exclaimed Pharaoh. "Young man, what's your name?"

"Joseph, your Majesty."

"Joseph," continued Pharaoh, "I will appoint you the new manager of my storehouses since you are the one who told me the meaning of my dreams. Your God must be with you in a special way!"

When Joseph walked away, he still could not believe Pharaoh's words. How could things happen so fast? After all those years in prison he had suddenly become the second most important man in Egypt, next to Pharaoh himself!

But Joseph did not fully realize that when God raises a man to honor and responsibility, He does not do it overnight. It takes time. For Joseph it took many years. Joseph was a good man who had learned to honor God for His blessings.

More than thirteen years had passed since the day Joseph was thrown in the well by his brothers. In that time he had become the governor of Egypt, second only to Pharaoh. He wore the royal signet ring, and when he drove his royal chariot through the streets, people bowed to him and called him "Sire."

And it had happened exactly as Joseph had foretold. First came the seven good years with plenty to eat. Joseph had stored millions of tons of grain in the royal storehouses for the bad years to come. Then, despite the years of famine, there was enough food for the people in Egypt. But the countries around Egypt suffered greatly.

Back in the land of Canaan, Jacob and his sons had barely enough to eat. The grass was gone. The wells had dried up. Jacob's green fields had become desert.

Every day Jacob's sons came home with worse news than the day before. "Forty more sheep died today!" reported Reuben one day. "I'm sorry father, but this can't go on."

"Well, don't just stand there!" scolded Jacob. "Do something! Why don't you go to Egypt? I told you there's food in Egypt. I heard it from a caravan last month. Go and buy some grain before we die like the sheep in the field. Hurry up! But, in case something should happen to you, I don't want Benjamin to get hurt. Benjamin stays home with me!"

When the ten brothers arrived at the storehouses of Egypt, they were brought before the governor, who was Joseph. Of course they did not recognize their little brother. He had become a man. He wore beautiful clothes. He looked like a prince. Even his name had been changed from Joseph to Zaphenath-paneah. They bowed before him and told him about the famine in the land of Canaan.

But Joseph recognized his brothers. As they bowed down before him, he remembered the dreams he had dreamt as a child. But he decided not to reveal who he was. He even pretended he did not understand his brothers' language. Everything they said had to be translated into the Egyptian language.

"I don't believe you," he replied harshly when the brothers had told their story. He wanted to test them. "I think you are spies from the land of Canaan. You intend to bring an army against Egypt, and that's why you have come disguised as farmers!"

"Your Honor," said Simeon, "that's not true! We have come to Egypt to buy grain. We are brothers, not spies. Our father sent us."

"No," repeated Joseph. "You are spies!"

"Sir," pleaded Simeon, "I assure you we tell the truth! Our father sent us to buy grain."

"Who is your father then?"

"Our father is Jacob, also called Israel, from Hebron in the land of Canaan. He had twelve sons. One of them is dead, the other one stayed home with him. We are the remaining ten sons."

"Hmm," said Joseph, "we'll see whether you speak the truth or not."

Then he had the ten brothers put in prison for three days. "I want them to know what an Egyptian prison is like," he thought to himself.

24

After three days he told the ten brothers, "I've made my decision. You may buy grain and take it back to Canaan. But I want to put you to the test in order to see if you spoke the truth. I will keep one of you in prison as a hostage while the other nine of you go home and bring your little brother back to me."

At Joseph's words Simeon turned to his brothers. "Oh no," he said in their own language, thinking Joseph could not understand. "Father will never allow that. I think we're in trouble. We are getting what we deserve. God is punishing us because we sold Joseph as a slave. Do you remember how he cried out when we sold him for twenty silver pieces? But we didn't listen. We can thank ourselves for the mess we're in now."

"Yes," said Reuben, the oldest brother. "Didn't I tell you it was wrong? Why didn't you listen to me?"

"Please Reuben," interrupted Simeon. "You've said that a thousand times. You go back to our father with the rest of our brothers and ask to bring Benjamin back with you. I'll stay here as the governor's hostage."

"But Father will never let Benjamin go," whispered Judah sadly.

Joseph listened while his brothers talked. He found it difficult to hold back his tears. He felt pity and sorrow for his brothers. Of course he had understood every word they said. He hurried outside and wept by himself. Now he knew his brothers felt sorry for what they had done.

But still, he did not let them know who he was. First he wanted to see his little brother Benjamin.

ather Jacob was angry when he heard their message. "Why did you even tell the Egyptian governor you had another brother at home?" he shouted at his sons. "You want to go back to Egypt and take Benjamin, my dead Rachel's Benjamin, with you? I can never let that happen!"

"But father," said Reuben, "we must go back! Simeon is being held hostage in Egypt. The governor will not release him unless we bring Benjamin. I promise you, we will bring Benjamin safely back to you. You may take my own two sons if we don't!"

"Look!" Levi interrupted them. He was unpacking the donkeys with the sacks of grain from Egypt. "Here's the money purse which I gave in return for the grain, lying right on top!"

"My money is here, too!" shouted his brother Gad. Now the other brothers untied their sacks. On top of each sack of grain was the money they were supposed to have paid for it.

"I don't understand this!" said Reuben. "I'm sure we paid. What will the governor of Egypt think when he realizes we brought our money back with us? He may punish Simeon for it! Father, we have to go back!"

Even though the nine brothers wanted to return to Egypt and take Benjamin with them, Jacob was firm. "No!" he commanded.

He knew he might never see Simeon again, but he would not trade Benjamin for Simeon.

A year passed. Finally Jacob realized he had no choice. He would have to send his sons back to Egypt to buy more grain. One morning, after all the grain had been eaten and they had been starving for days, Jacob said to his sons, "Go back to Egypt and buy more grain."

"All right father," answered Judah, "but you know we have to take Benjamin along with us. The governor may kill all of us if we show up without him."

"I'll give you plenty of money to pay for the grain," retorted Jacob.

"We still must take Benjamin with us," repeated Judah.

"Very well," sighed Jacob. "But no harm must come to him! Take a double amount of silver with you to pay for both the new grain and the grain you got last time. Here, take these gifts for the governor as well, balm, honey, myrrh and spices . . . and pistachio nuts and almonds."

So the brothers trudged back down to Egypt once again.

And this time Benjamin went with them.

Joseph, the governor, greeted them sternly. "What took you so long? Is this the youngest brother?"

Joseph looked carefully at the newcomer. He knew it was Benjamin! Oh, how he had missed his little brother! He wanted to hug him and tell him who he was. He wanted to kiss him and talk to him as in the old days. But he dared not, not yet.

Instead he invited his brothers to eat with him in his own house, still not revealing who he was.

"How is your father?" Joseph asked the brothers at the table. "Is he still alive?"

So they told him about their aged father and the trouble they all were in because of the famine in Canaan. While they were eating and speaking, Joseph thought of a plan.

The next morning he told his servants to load the brothers' donkeys with food. "Now listen carefully," he continued to his servant. "Put each man's silver on top of the grain just like the last time. Then take my precious silver cup and lay it together with the money in the youngest brother's sack."

"But . . . ," said the servant.

"Just do exactly as I say," commanded Joseph.

On their way back to Canaan the brothers were happy and cheerful. Both Benjamin and Simeon were with them. They sang and joked as they drove their loaded donkeys north toward Hebron.

"Great fellow, this governor, huh?" shouted Judah.

"Yes," Reuben shouted back. "He's not as tough as I thought!"

"Did you know," said Levi, who was the cleverest one of them all, "most Egyptians would never dream of eating with a Hebrew? Still, the governor invited us to eat at his very own table!"

"I even began to like him," laughed Reuben.

Suddenly, as one of the brothers turned around, he noticed a dust cloud on the horizon behind them. The cloud slowly grew. They realized they were being followed by Egyptian soldiers. The soldiers caught up with them, jumped off their horses and commanded, "Stop in the name of Pharaoh!"

"What's the matter?" protested Reuben. He stepped between the soldiers and the brothers.

"The governor's silver cup has disappeared," answered the captain in charge. "The governor has sent us to see if one of you stole it."

"Stole it?" exclaimed Reuben. "I assure you . . . ."

"Open your bags!" interrupted the captain. He had the brothers stand in a long line, Reuben first, Benjamin last. When he came to Benjamin he dug his arm down into the sack and triumphantly raised the sparkling silver cup over his head.

"Oh no," said Judah. "Benjamin stole the governor's silver cup! I can't believe it!"

"Benjamin!" said Reuben. "What have you done?"

But Benjamin just stared at the silver cup. He had no idea how it had ended up in his sack.

"You are under arrest!" said the captain, grabbing Benjamin by the shoulder. Then he turned to the other brothers. "You must all follow me back to the governor's house," he said.

So they loaded their donkeys again, turned around and went slowly back to the city.

Joseph was waiting at home for his brothers to be brought back. By putting the silver cup in Benjamin's sack he had made sure he had a good reason to arrest Benjamin. He intended to let the other brothers go home and keep only Benjamin, his dear little brother.

"What have you done to me?" he said sternly to the brothers standing in front of him. "You . . . yes you . . . Benjamin, you stole my silver cup!"

Benjamin trembled. He had not done it. He knew that. How could the governor's silver cup have ended up in his sack? Benjamin noticed the way the governor pronounced his name. For a fraction of a second it reminded him of his lost brother Joseph, with whom he had played in the fields of Hebron as a small boy.

"I'm putting your youngest brother under arrest!" continued the governor. "He'll be a slave in Egypt for the rest of his life. But all of you are free to go back to your country."

"Your Honor," Judah cried, "allow me to speak a word. If Benjamin doesn't return with us, our father will die from sorrow. He cannot bear to lose his youngest son. He has already lost one. Please let me take Benjamin's place and be your slave instead."

Joseph looked at his brothers. They were all in tears. Tears appeared in his own eyes. He bit his lip trying to control his expression, but it was no use.

"Servants," he commanded, "leave me alone with these Hebrew men!"

The tears rolled down his cheeks as he stepped closer and took off his Egyptian headdress.

"Joseph!" gasped Benjamin.

"Benjamin!" wept Joseph as he hugged his younger brother. Then Joseph went from brother to brother and named them by their Hebrew names as he kissed them. For a long time no words were spoken, but the weeping of the twelve united brothers was heard throughout the governor's house.

Finally Joseph said, "Brothers, do not regret what you did to me when you sold me as a slave many years ago. God has been with me and turned my troubles into a blessing. How I've longed to share my blessings with you. Now, go back to our father and to your families and bring them down to Egypt. Yes, and bring all your possessions and cattle and sheep. I will prepare a place for you with plenty of grain and water. I want you to be guests of Pharaoh and Egypt."

Joseph's childhood dreams had come true. He had become the most powerful man in the world, next to King Pharaoh himself. He had become so mighty, even his own brothers had bowed before him.

But not only had Joseph's dreams come true. God's purpose for him came true as well. Through Joseph's faithfulness when times were hard, and his endurance in prison, Joseph had learned to see that his blessings came from God. In this way he became a man capable of handling his big dreams. He had become a man of compassion and humility, able to forget himself and reach out to those around him.

So, when Joseph's father finally came to Egypt and bowed before his son, Joseph pulled him to his feet and hugged him.

"Welcome, father!" he whispered.

You can find the story of Joseph in the Old Testament in the Book of Genesis, chapters 37-50.